Golf- This damn Sport !

One Hundred Seven Ways to Shoot 107

By Harold Bluestein, PGA

CONTENTS

ACKNOWLEDGEMENTS

Grateful thanks to: Golf enthusiasts, tour professionals and celebrities for their wise and witty quotes included in this book.

Thanks to my old friend and college fraternity brother Alan Levine for his edits.

I want to thank my sons David and Daniel and daughter Katie for not regretting their childhood with a golf pro.

Most of all I want to thank my beautiful wife Susie. She has been with me for every chip, chunk, shank and misspelling along the way.

Harold Bluestein

FOREWORD

I laughed so hard reading Harold's "Golf- This damn Sport!"

I lost track of time.

I know you'll love it too.

Peter Jacobsen

PGA Tour/Champions Tour

Golf Channel, NBC Analyst

INTRODUCTION

In my long career as a PGA Golf Professional I've witnessed hundreds of funny golf moments. I share the same ups and downs with everyone who's ever played this game. I've learned to accept my frustrations with a sense of humor. Because as maddening as this damn sport is, like you, I love it.

The subtitle of this book, "One Hundred Seven Ways to Shoot 107" is in direct conflict with published research claiming 55% of all golfers' score-less than100. My "official study" showed that when do-overs, errors in addition, and rules violations are taken into account only 10% of golfers have ever broken100, and most scored closer to 107!

"Golf – This damn Sport!" is a collection of 107 of my original cartoons and more than seventy celebrity quotes. The cartoons and quotes cover a variety of subjects including instruction, equipment, course management and marriage. My book illustrates all the craziness inherent in our hapless yet humorous golf moments on and off the course.

No matter how poorly our swing performs or how high our scores climb we embrace our golf obsession and reserve another tee time.

Harold Bluestein, PGA

Chapter 1

Shooting 107 takes time

Strokes 1 through 9

Your day starts with the best intentions. You anticipate a record round of golf.

But anything can happen on your way to shooting 107.

You didn't plan on your slice rearing its ugly head. Why would your GPS wrist watch display yardage to the wrong green? Where did all those ball-swallowing ponds come from?

Your self-confidence melted like an ice cube on a hot day.

Hey Mom, delay dinner.
This could take a while.

Stroke #1

Stroke #2

Stroke #3

Now *that's* a mean slice.

Stroke #4

I'll shoot my age if I live to be 105.

Bob Hope

I was laying 10 and had a 35-foot putt. I whispered over my shoulder to my caddie: "How does this one break?" He replied: "Who cares."

Jack Lemmon

My best score ever is 103. But I've only been playing 15 years.

Alex Karras

Sure it was a bad shot Fred, but
eventually you will have to get up.

Stroke #5

He's between clubs - his 3 wood
and his sand wedge.

Stroke #6

From 150 yards the eight-iron is *absolutely* the right club for you. Hit it three times.

Stroke #7

I'm hitting the woods just great, but I'm having a terrible time getting out of them.

Harry Toscano

If we don't hurry up the group behind us will want to play through for the second time.

Harold Bluestein

It took me seventeen years to get three thousand hits in baseball. I did it in one afternoon on the golf course.

Hank Aaron

As if a 15 wasn't amazing. Hitting the same tree with your third, seventh and twelfth shots was remarkable!

Stroke #8

Re-routing

Stroke #9

Chapter 2

Golf clubs are "ill-designed for the purpose"

Strokes 10 through 18

You praise your clubs when they hit the ball straight. You scold them when they squirt the ball "sideways." Every one of your clubs has a mind of its own!

No matter how much you plead, your five-iron refuses to get airborne. It's not your fault the driver can't find the fairway or the putter misses the hole.

You *are* the Royal Golf Club Executioner. When your clubs misbehave you can break them, toss them in a creek or park them in a dark corner of the garage.

Yes – but the way I putt, it could hardly be considered a deadly weapon.

Stroke #10

The pro said we were a
match made in heaven but evidently
someone doesn't agree.

Stroke #11

New driver?

Stroke #12

Wait Harry! I was wrong.
You didn't make 14. It was a 13.

Stroke #13

When I'm on the course and it starts to rain and lightning, I hold up my one iron, 'cause I know even God can't hit a one iron.

Lee Trevino

Golf is a game whose aim is to hit a very small ball into an even smaller hole, with weapons singularly ill-designed for the purpose.

Sir Winston Churchill

I've thrown a few clubs in my day. I guess at one time or another I probably held distance records for every club in the bag.

Tommy Bolt

Stroke #14

Stroke #15

Either you deliver a new driver Christmas morning or I reveal your *true* identity - Bernie Schwartz, part-time pharmacist.

Stroke #16

Never break your putter and your driver in the same round.

Tommy Bolt

My putter had a heart attack the last nine holes and just died on me.

Lanny Wadkins

I was always more of a breaker than a thrower - most of them putters. I broke so many of those; I probably became the world's foremost authority on how to putt without a putter.

Tommy Bolt

There's probably an app for that.

Stroke #17

That putter is absolutely, positively guaranteed to work for a week.

Stroke #18

Chapter 3

It takes balls to play this game

Strokes 19 through 27

You remember a time standing on the tee with water right, out of bounds left and only one ball left in your bag.

You had to borrow a ball to finish your round! How embarrassing.

Now your golf bag bulges with an eclectic collection of balls. But you still risk life and limb searching for the one you bought from the neighbor kid for 50 cents.

Who says it takes balls to play golf?

Stroke #19

The embarrassment of ball shopping

Stroke #20

For you I recommend a 2 piece ball
with a bolognamer cover and
an unobtainium core.

Stroke #21

See it on that rock?
I wouldn't ask Ralph; but you're the
smallest, fastest and it's my *last* ball.

Stroke #22

I can airmail the golf ball, but sometimes
I don't put the right address on it.

Jim Dent

It's good sportsmanship not to pick up
lost balls while they are still moving.

Mark Twain

One of the advantages bowling has over
golf is that you seldom lose a bowling ball.

Don Carter

Get up! Go! Draw! Fade! Sit!
Make up your mind.

Stroke #23

Beaten, cursed at and lost.
And you say I'm overreacting!?

Stroke #24

See mine don't have a logo on them.

Stroke #25

If you think it's hard to meet new people, try picking up the wrong golf ball.

Jack Lemmon

Sometimes when I look down at that little white golf ball, I wish it was moving.

Dusty Baker

If profanity had an influence on the flight of the ball the game of golf would be played far better than it is.

Horace Hutchinson

Stroke #26

Stroke #27

Chapter 4

For better or worse until death do us part

Strokes 28 through 36

You know playing golf with your significant other can be a challenge.

Say too much: "You've made it too complicated." Say too little: "You're no help at all!"

When asked: "Why am I topping the ball?" You *know* it's a trap from which you cannot escape.

But you can't help yourself.

Anything more you'd like to add honey?

Stroke #28

That's the *third* time. Maybe we should let our wives play through.

Stroke #29

My wife would rather I didn't play the back nine.

Stroke #30

Stroke #31

He quit playing when
I started out driving him.

Joanne Carner
referring to her husband

My wife and I are at a point in our
marriage where we can play nine
holes without either one of us crying.

Harold Bluestein

When I die, bury me on the golf
course so my husband will visit.

Author Unknown

Now will you ask where the 10th tee is?

Stroke #32

Stroke #33

Stroke #34

I lost 150 pounds if you include my wife.

David Feherty

It's a marriage. If I had to choose between my wife and my putter – I'd miss her.

Gary Player

Golf and sex are about the only things you can enjoy without being good at it.

Jimmy Demaret

When I die bury my balls next to the old bag.

Author Unknown

Okay...Okay...Next time
I'll give you *four* shots a side.

Stroke #35

I said: "Take the drop Harry!" But no....

Stroke #36

Chapter 5

It's more than just a game

Strokes 37 through 45

How many times have you said, "I'm terrible, I suck at golf," but keep hitting practice balls until your back ached?

You've popped a couple ibuprofens, waited out a three-hour frost delay hoping for a chance to bathe in the glow of golfing success.

When you're on the course every cell in your body is wrapped up in the challenge. Hit that special shot, you feel alive. Hit a terrible shot, your heart sinks to your feet.

Golf is more than just a game; it's your Mount Everest.

Warm-up, minor adjustment or the extreme makeover bucket?

Stroke #37

Some of them can live
all winter long on stored up fat.

Stroke #38

Okay Grandpa, double or nothing?

Stroke #39

Charlie in Accounting wants your putter.
Buzz in Sales has dibs on your driver.
Should I cancel your tee time for tomorrow?

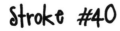

They call it golf because all the other four-letter words were taken.

Raymond Floyd

I'm going to miss at least seven shots in every eighteen holes, so if I'm going to be angry, I might as well start on the first hole.

Walter Hagen

I told him he was one year away from the Tour and next year he'll be two years away.

Chi Chi Rodriguez

Stroke #41

Stroke #42

Frost Delay

Stroke #43

I never had a good bounce.
All I ever had were bad ones.

Arnold Palmer

The way I hit the ball today
I need to go to the range.
Instead I think I'll go to the bar.

Fuzzy Zoeller

If you're going to throw a club, it is
important to throw it ahead of you,
down the fairway, so you don't waste
energy going back to pick it up.

Tommy Bolt

It's always best to let the boss win.

Stroke #44

Don't think of it as a 5 putt Fred.
Think of it as an 8.

Stroke #45

Chapter 6

What could possibly go wrong?

Strokes 46 through 54

Your round is a swing away from a disaster lurking around the next dogleg or over the next hill.

Mental coaches' preach your reaction to failure impacts your success as a golfer. But you wonder how many of those gurus followed two double bogeys with a triple bogey and kept smiling?

You'd like to take golf's mental game experts' advice when your ball gets buried in a bunker, or a playing partner shanks his ball into your groin.

But it won't be easy.

Sure we're playing bad, but
I didn't think it had come to this.

Stroke #46

Wow! That was my most solid hit yet.

Stroke #47

Sorry about the shank Fred. Can I use your new driver while you're laid up?

Stroke #48

Do I *look* like a motivational speaker?

Stroke #49

Whenever I play with him, I usually try to make it a foursome - the President, myself, a paramedic and a faith healer.

Bob Hope on Gerald Ford

I should have played that hole in an ambulance.

Arnold Palmer

When the squirrels and birds see us on the tee, they start scattering. We've set back the mating season in Texas 90 days.

John Plumbley

It's possible I misunderstood him when he said he wanted to be six under.

Stroke #50

It won't be long now.

Stroke #51

With super human commitment and will-power, you should be able to quit this game in two weeks.

Stroke #52

I'm awful sorry honey [woman hit on the backside] but I'd had 30 more yards if you had gotten out of the way.

Former Speaker of the House
Tip O'Neill

Flags on the greens should be at half-staff.

Al Maletesta

If this was a prize fight, they'd stopped it.

Bob Hope

Nearly half way to 107 – 9 holes enough?

Stroke #53

Anyone see a ball come through here?

Stroke #54

Chapter 7

In search of the miraculous

Strokes 55 through 63

You have a library of "how to" golf books, DVD's and subscribe to a half dozen golf magazines. You run the Golf Channel 24/7.

Nothing works.

Whether golf's magic formula is hidden under a rock on a Scottish golf course, painted on a cave wall in southern France or simply camouflaged in plain sight you *know* it exists.

We moved golf books from SPORTS to SELF HELP, then to FICTION, before settling on MYSTERY.

Stroke #55

This is absolutely, positively the
last training aid you will ever need.

Stroke #56

Shhh…
He's preparing for the upcoming season.

Stroke #57

Tennis…

Stroke #58

I don't have any big secret about putting…
Just hit at it. It's either going to miss or go in.

Ben Crenshaw

My putting was atrocious. I changed
my grips, stance, you name it. I tried
everything but standing on my head.

Arnold Palmer

He enjoys that perfect peace, that peace
beyond all understanding, which comes
at its maximum only to the man who has
given up golf.

P.G. Wodehouse

Help ??

Stroke #59

Stroke #60

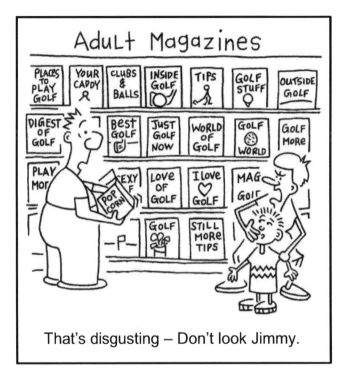

That's disgusting – Don't look Jimmy.

Stroke #61

I'm about five inches from being an outstanding golfer. That's the distance my left ear is from my right.

Ben Crenshaw

We've got a society now looking for answers anywhere. They might go to a car wash to take a lesson.

Jackie Burke Jr

I don't trust doctors. They're like golfers. Everyone has a different answer to your problem.

Seve Ballesteros

Hit 2 of these and call me in the morning.

Stroke #62

There are an infinite number of ways to hit a golf ball Mr. Muldoon. Try one of them.

Stroke #63

Chapter 8

Can history teach us anything?

Strokes 64 through 72

People throughout history have been fascinated with stick and ball games. Some like baseball. Others prefer hockey. Your choice is golf.

You share the same skill and level of frustration as the Scots who invented this game 400 years ago; albeit they were kings, queens and archers.

They scattered boiled-feather-filled-balls with hickory sticks around the sheep-shorn heather countryside. You scatter three-piece-balls with graphite clubs around machine-manicured grass fairways.

Except for the equipment and the length of the grass nothing much has changed.

Wait!! Does it say anything about curing a slice?

Stroke #64

First golfing vacation Harry?

Stroke #65

Eight iron? You sure that's enough club?

Stroke #66

Sisyphus takes up golf.

Stroke #67

Golf is a good walk spoiled.

Mark Twain

Columbus went around the world in 1492. That is not a lot of strokes when you consider the course.

Lee Trevino

Golf is a game kings and presidents play when they get tired of running countries.

Charles Price

Stroke #68

Stroke #69

Stroke #70

Golf is a game invented by the same people who think music comes from a bagpipe.

Lee Trevino

Golf is not a game, its bondage. It was obviously devised by a man torn with guilt, eager to atone for his sins.

Jim Murray

Until you play it, St Andrews looks like the sort of real estate you couldn't give away.

Sam Snead

It was an ancient form of self-deprecation.

Stroke #71

I know your clubs are outdated because the signature on them is *A. Lincoln*.

Stroke #72

Chapter 9

Let this be a lesson

Strokes 73 through 81

You've tried every swing method known to man. Your self-prescribed approach to a perfect golf swing hasn't worked.

This game is supposed to be fun and rewarding. It would be if you could find a little consistency. Pros take lessons but they're "consistently good" while you're "consistently bad." They want to hit more greens. You want to hit fewer trees.

Is there anyone out there who can get all your moving body parts coordinated to hit a golf ball straight?

Wow Mr. Lehmann!
You really *stuck* that landing.

Stroke #73

Perhaps we should work on your grip.

Stroke #74

That's excellent Mr. Lewis. Now let's try chewing your gum at the same time.

Stroke #75

So… Was that a chip or a pitch?

Stroke #76

Golf is a game in which a ball, one and a half inches in diameter is placed on a ball 8,000 miles in diameter. The object is to hit the small ball but not the larger.

John Cunningham

Ninety percent of putts that are short never go in.

Yogi Berra

Your swing has more planes than Boeing.

Harold Bluestein
assessing a new student

That was a fine swing Mrs. Kopecky.
Next week we'll work on your balance.

Stroke #77

Very encouraging! You hit 100 range balls
and didn't fall down on the last two.

Stroke #78

WELCOME TO JUNIOR GOLF CAMP

PRO

Eight year olds with
a personal trainer but not yet
signed with an agent over there.

Stroke #79

If people gripped a knife and fork like
they do a golf club, they'd starve to death.

Sam Snead

I've seen better swings on
a condemned playground.

Arnold Palmer

If you want to hit your 8-iron further,
it's called a 7-iron.

Harold Bluestein

Your golf pro helped me pick it out.

Stroke #80

I'm better prepared for your lesson *this* time Mrs. Burnbottom.

Stroke #81

Chapter 10

Managing misadventures

Strokes 82 through 90

How many times have you been cruising along nicely on the golf course and out of nowhere you hit a bump in the road.

It calls for a split-second decision. Make the right decision and the next couple minutes could be great. Make the wrong one and the rest of the round could be a disaster.

Fortunately for you, years of facing golf's adversities have given you tools to deal with misadventures. You can handle anything this damn game throws at you.

And if things get really bad, there's 911.

Hello pro shop? Can you hear me?
I may be in a dead zone.

Stroke #82

Stroke #83

Stroke #84

Stroke #85

I may go for it or I may not. It all depends on what I elect to do on my backswing.

Billy Joe Patton

That was a great shot – if they'd put the pin there today.

David Feherty

Golf is a lot of walking, broken up by disappointment and bad arithmetic.

Author Unknown

I'd been in a lot of bunkers - my caddie told me he was getting blisters from raking so much.

Joanne Carner

Stroke #86

Stroke #87

Stroke #88

Forward the check to charity to help offset the cost of all the condo windows I broke during my play today.

Gary McCord

If I'da cleared the trees and drove the green, it woulda been a great tee shot.

Sam Snead

Like they say in golf, if you aim for nothing, you'll hit it every time.

Yogi Berra

I was vacuuming right along when
I ran into *Rule 16.1 - Abnormal Conditions,
Immovable Obstructions.*

Stroke #89

Okay Phil, you're away.

Stroke #90

Chapter 11

Golf conundrums

Strokes 91 through 99

Golf is puzzling to you. There are obscure rules, challenging weather conditions and weird playing partners.

Your round doesn't follow any logical pattern. It's organized chaos. Boom a birdie! Boom a triple bogey! Oops a quad, dammit!

Yet for some inexplicable reason, you love it.

Yes … But it's a *dry* heat.

Stroke #91

Stroke #92

Stroke #93

Stroke #94

It's hard to keep score like I do with someone looking over your shoulder.

Bob Hope

The less you bet the more you lose when you win.

Jim Snider

It [par] can be anything I want it to be. For instance this hole right here is a par 47 and yesterday I birdied the sucker.

Willie Nelson

It's a trifecta Stan.
Your blood pressure, cholesterol
and golf scores are all the same.

Stroke #95

There's something intimidating
about a woman with a rule book.

Stroke #96

To keep today's round *our* little secret you'll have to dig a little deeper.

Stroke #97

The older you are the longer you used to be.

Chi Chi Rodriguez

I used to play golf with a guy who cheated so badly that he once had a hole-in-one and wrote down zero on his scorecard.

Bob Bruce

Golf is more fun than walking naked in a strange place, but not much.

Buddy Hackett

Stroke #98

Stroke #99

Chapter 12

When the going gets tough, the tough keep playing
Strokes 100 through 107

If it wasn't the furthest point from the clubhouse you would have walked off the golf course. But you're not a quitter.

You erase from your mind the missed twelve-inch putt on the previous hole.

The sun beats down on your balding head. Your hands shake and your eyes water. Someone in the group behind you yells – "hit it already!"

Like a battle-scarred veteran of the PGA tour you steady your $300 putter.
You call on years of nightly practice on the spare bedroom carpet for a stroke to restore your self-respect.

Looks like you could use a 4 ounce "Bombs Away, High Performance Energy Boost".

Stroke #100

Hang in there Harriet.
Winter's behind us. I see the condo!

Stroke #101

Come onnnnnn…!!!

Stroke #102

Beans for lunch Mr. Whitson?

Stroke #103

The greater the bet, the longer the short putts become.

Author Unknown

The wind was so strong there were whitecaps in the porta-john.

Joyce Kazmierski

It is nothing new or original to say that golf is played one stroke at a time. But it took me many strokes to realize it.

Bobby Jones

When we were young we looked for *hip places* to play. Now we need *hip replacements* to play.

Stroke #104

How can they beat me? I've been Struck by lightning, had two back operations and been divorced twice.

Lee Trevino

If you watch a game, it's fun.
If you play it, it's recreation.
If you work at it, it's golf.

Bob Hope

My car absolutely will not run unless my golf clubs are in the trunk.

Bruce Berlet

Stroke #105

Stroke #106

13

Shank, yip,
another shank, chunk,
12!

15

Need sand wedge
left in the
bunker on #3

17

Can still break 100 but
need to borrow a ball

18

Oops 107 - Better
luck next week

Stroke #107

PARTING SHOTS

I play in the low 80s.
If it's any hotter than that, I won't play.

Joe E. Lewis

I have a tip that can take five strokes off
anyone's golf game. It's called an eraser.

Arnold Palmer

Golf is a game in which you yell 'fore',
shoot six, and write down five.

Paul Harvey

Good golfing temperament falls
between taking it with a grin
or a shrug and throwing a fit.

Sam Snead

ABOUT THE AUTHOR

Harold Bluestein played his first round of golf as a nine year old at the Audubon Golf Course in Williamsville, New York. Using his father's Johnny Bulla golf clubs he smashed, slashed and swatted his way to a love affair with golf.

He graduated from Kent State University with a degree in Political Science. After a brief construction career he decided to try his hand in the golf business. He started at the bottom as "caddie master/4th assistant" at Blue Hills Country Club in Kansas City, Missouri.

Harold has served as a PGA Head Professional, Director of Instruction and college golf coach. He is currently a radio co-host on 1080 The Fan's "Golf in the Northwest" and Oregon Chapter President of the Pacific Northwest Section PGA.

He is a six time winner of Northwest PGA Section Awards for his contributions to the PGA and regional golf community. Harold won an *Artist's Magazine All-Media Competition Grand Prize* for his fine art and a *Washington Newspaper Publishers Association Best Editorial Cartoon Award*.

Harold continues to play golf as a professional. His goals are to complete a round injury free and to shoot scores close to his age.